LIFE IN STRANGE PLACES

The Zoo on You

life on human skin

Harry Breidahl

This edition first published in 2002 in the United States of America by Chelsea House Publishers,
a subsidiary of Haights Cross Communications.

Chelsea House Publishers
1974 Sproul Road, Suite 400
Broomall, PA 19008-0914

The Chelsea House world wide web address is www.chelseahouse.com

Library of Congress Cataloging-in-Publication Data Applied for.
ISBN 0-7910-6619-3

First published in 2001 by
Macmillan Education Australia Pty Ltd
627 Chapel Street, South Yarra, Australia, 3141

Copyright © Harry Breidahl 2001

Edited by Angelique Campbell-Muir
Text design by Cristina Neri
Cover design by Cristina Neri
Desktop publishing by Katharine Shade and Cristina Neri
Illustrations by Rhyll Plant
Printed in China

Acknowledgements
The author and the publishers are grateful to the following for permission to reproduce copyright material:

Cover photographs: Leather background, courtesy PhotoDisc; tick, courtesy Photolibrary.com/Roberts
Brons/BPS; human body louse, courtesy Photolibrary.com/David Scharf/SPL.

Auscape/VEM-BSIP, pp. 5 (bottom left), 20; Australian Picture Library/Corbis, p. 28; Mary Evans Picture
Library, p. 29 (top right); PhotoDisc, pp. 5 (top right), 16, 22, 27 (bottom); Photolibrary.com/Andrew
Syred/SPL, pp. 17, 23; Photolibrary.com/David Scharf/SPL, pp. 1, 3, 8, 13 (both), 19 (right);
Photolibrary.com/Dr. P. Marazzi/SPL, p. 15 (bottom); Photolibrary.com/Eye of Science/SPL, pp. 4 (top), 11;
Photolibrary.com/Jane Shemilt/SPL, pp. 5 (top left), 19 (top left); Photolibrary.com/Philippe Plailly/SPL,
pp. 6–7 (top), 25; Photolibrary.com/Quest/SPL, p. 9; Photolibrary.com/Roberts Brons/BPS, p. 21;
Photolibrary.com/Science Photo Library, pp. 18–19 (bottom); Stephen Doggett/Department of Medical
Entomology, Westmead Hospital, pp. 4 (bottom), 5 (bottom right), 7, 11, 15 (top), 24, 26, 27 (top),
29 (bottom left).

Contents

SEARCHING THE WORLD WIDE WEB

If you have access to the world wide web, you usually have a gateway to some fascinating information. At this time, though, there is not a lot of information about the human zoo on the web. Nevertheless, if you search very carefully you should be able to find some useful information. In this book, useful search words appear like this— 🡕 head lice. Useful books and web sites are also listed on page 30.

Introducing the zoo on you

When people talk of wildlife they are usually referring to big things such as lions in Africa, kangaroos in Australia or, perhaps, a moose in North America. These are all large and easily recognized animals.

There are also many small creatures—some so tiny that we can only see them through a microscope. Nevertheless, it is true, your skin can support a veritable 'zoo' of weird and wonderful wildlife.

Lice are only a couple of millimeters long, but they are the largest members of the human zoo. The best known of these are the ⚐ head lice. (See pages 10–13.)

Mites are tiny eight-legged relatives of spiders. One kind of mite lives in human **hair follicles**. Another kind can burrow under human skin. (See pages 14–17).

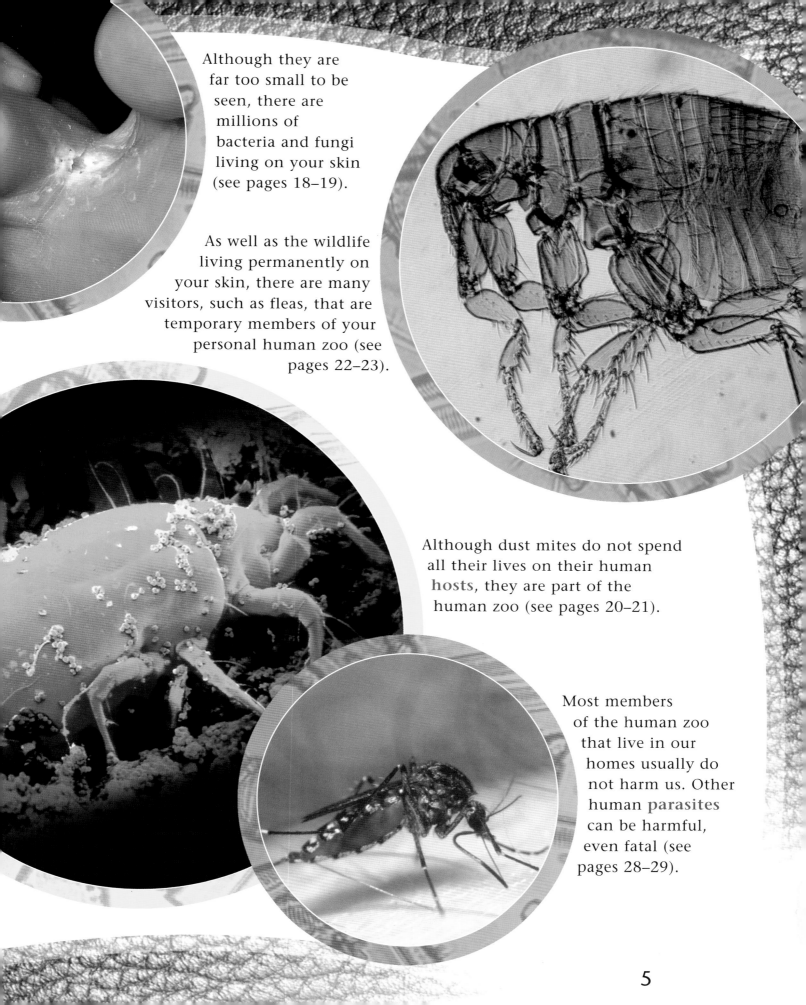

Although they are far too small to be seen, there are millions of bacteria and fungi living on your skin (see pages 18–19).

As well as the wildlife living permanently on your skin, there are many visitors, such as fleas, that are temporary members of your personal human zoo (see pages 22–23).

Although dust mites do not spend all their lives on their human **hosts**, they are part of the human zoo (see pages 20–21).

Most members of the human zoo that live in our homes usually do not harm us. Other human **parasites** can be harmful, even fatal (see pages 28–29).

Background
Measuring the human zoo

To get an idea of just how small some of the human zoo are, you first need to think about measurement. The measurement units used in this book belong to the **metric system**. In the metric system, the smallest commonly used unit is the millimeter (mm). (If you are used to feet and inches, 100 mm equals about 4 inches.) A human eye can see objects as small as one-tenth of a millimeter across—any smaller than that and you would need a magnifying glass or a microscope to see clearly.

Because the members of the human zoo are so small, you also need to be familiar with the units of measurement used for things that are smaller than a millimeter. This is where the metric system is easy to follow because each new unit is smaller by a factor of 10, 100 or 1000. Counting down in lots of 1000, there are three important metric units of measurement that you need to remember:

- one millimeter (mm) is $^1/1000$ of a meter
- one micrometer (µm) is $^1/1000$ of a millimeter
- one nanometer (nm) is $^1/1000$ of a micrometer.

human eye

1 mm
1000 µm

10 mm
1 cm

human flea

Illustrations not drawn to scale.

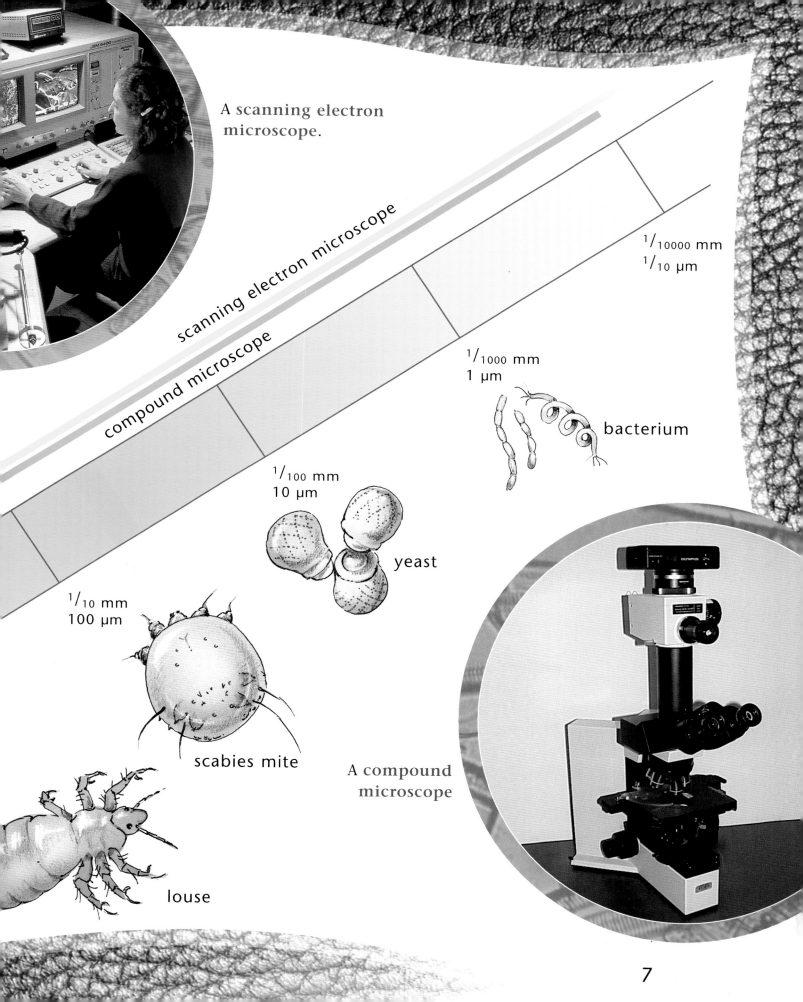

A scanning electron microscope.

scanning electron microscope

compound microscope

$^1/_{10000}$ mm
$^1/_{10}$ μm

$^1/_{1000}$ mm
1 μm

bacterium

$^1/_{100}$ mm
10 μm

yeast

$^1/_{10}$ mm
100 μm

scabies mite

A compound microscope

louse

Skin as a habitat

Your skin is a barrier between your body and the **environment**
The skin of an average adult human covers an area of around
6 square meters (20 square feet), and weighs about 3 kilograms
(6.6 pounds). Your skin is actually your largest **organ**, and it is
also the fastest growing. Your skin is made up of two layers—the
epidermis and the dermis. The epidermis is the outer layer of your
skin. The dermis is the layer under the epidermis.

The purpose of your skin is to act as a tough, flexible and
waterproof outer covering to your body. It helps to protect your
body against injury and infection, and from heat and sunlight.
This means that your skin is not an ideal **habitat**. Nevertheless,
just below the layer of dead cells that make up the outer surface
of your epidermis, is a rich supply of blood and other substances.
Parasites look for these things. So, no matter how hostile an
environment your skin might be, it is attractive to many types of
minute wildlife. Some live on you permanently, and others are
just visitors.

HOW DO YOU SAY IT?

dermis: **der**-mus
epidermis: epi-**der**-mus

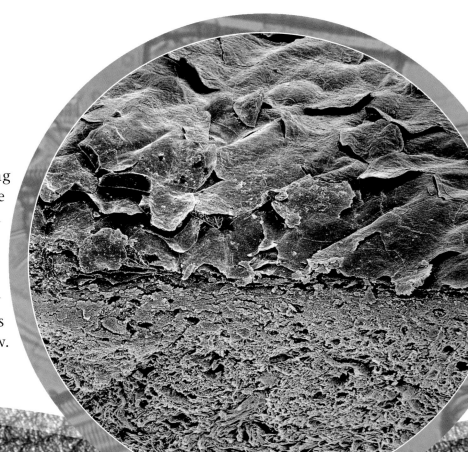

When seen through a scanning
electron microscope, the
outer surface of human skin
(epidermis) looks like a rocky
desert. This is because it is
made up of dead skin cells.
These dead cells are constantly
lost and replaced by new ones
from below.

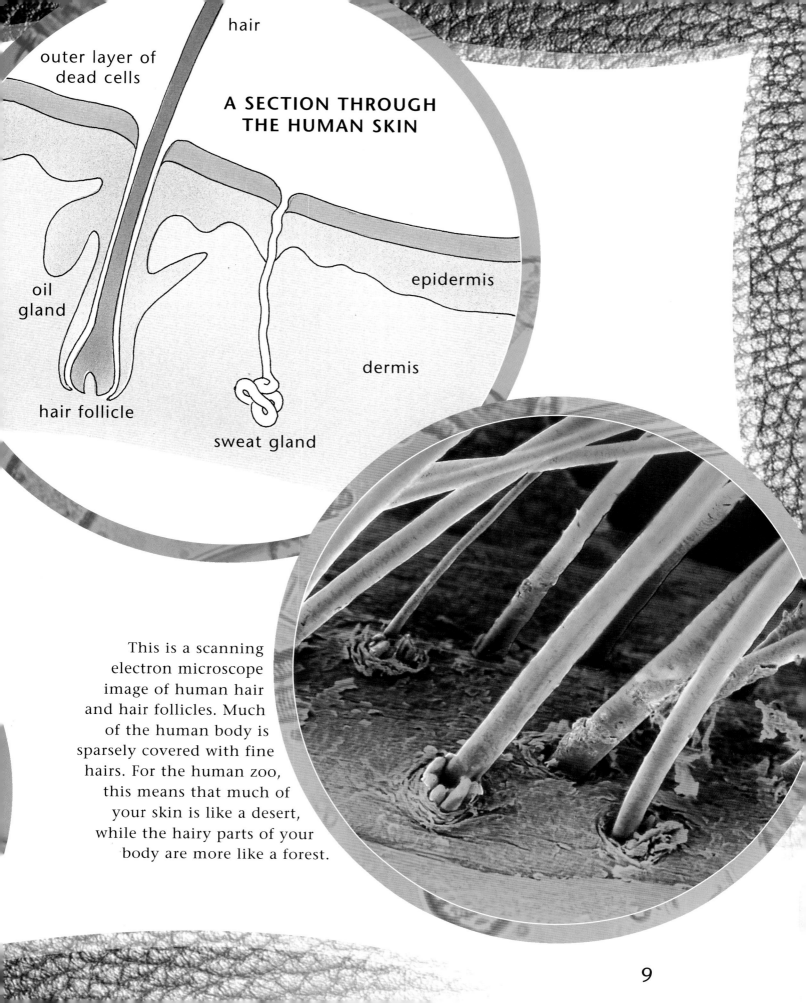

hair

outer layer of
dead cells

A SECTION THROUGH
THE HUMAN SKIN

epidermis

oil
gland

dermis

hair follicle

sweat gland

This is a scanning
electron microscope
image of human hair
and hair follicles. Much
of the human body is
sparsely covered with fine
hairs. For the human zoo,
this means that much of
your skin is like a desert,
while the hairy parts of your
body are more like a forest.

The human zoo
Head lice and nits

Head lice are probably the best known members of the human zoo. They can only survive in the hairy, forest-like part of your body—your head. You do not need a microscope to see a head louse, but a magnifying glass could be useful. That is because a head louse is between 2 and 3 millimeters long. A female louse can lay six to eight eggs per night, and up to 300 eggs in her lifetime. These eggs are called nits.

The thought of tiny insects wandering about your head may be repulsive, especially when you find that head lice feed on blood. A head louse can only survive if it feeds on human blood every day. Thankfully, head lice do not pose a major health problem. In fact, head lice can be quite common even in clean households and on people with clean hair.

HOW DO YOU SAY IT?

thorax: **thor**-axe

Nits are laid on a single strand of hair. They can be removed with a fine comb or careful 'nit picking'. Once head lice and nits are removed there should be no long-lasting health problems.

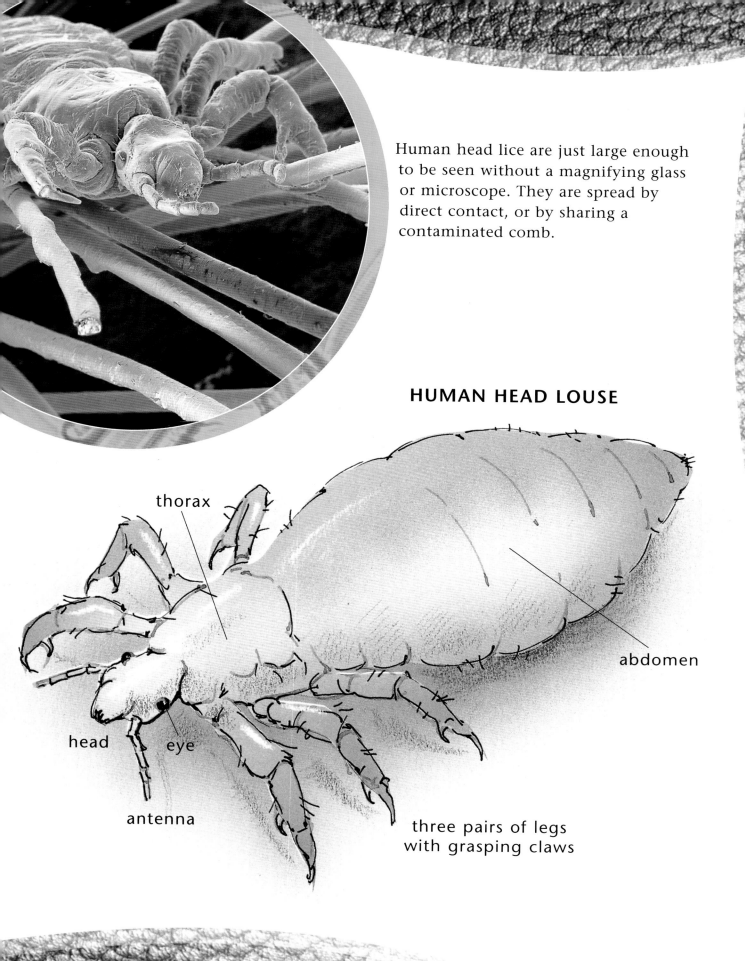

Human head lice are just large enough to be seen without a magnifying glass or microscope. They are spread by direct contact, or by sharing a contaminated comb.

HUMAN HEAD LOUSE

thorax

abdomen

head

eye

antenna

three pairs of legs
with grasping claws

Body lice

Almost all lice have adapted to live amongst the hair of an animal's body. Because the human body is relatively hairless, this may, at first, seem to rule out lice on our bodies. However, human 🔎 body lice have replaced the hairy bodies of our ancestors with the nearest thing available—the clothes we wear. 🔎 Crab lice are another kind of body lice that have adapted to living in our pubic hair.

Body lice were far more of a problem in the past than they are today. In the past, people who were infested with lice were said to be 'lousy'. Because we regularly wash our clothes and our bodies, body lice and crab lice are now uncommon. This is a relief because body lice feed on human blood and, unlike head lice, body lice are known to transmit fatal diseases.

HUMAN BODY LOUSE

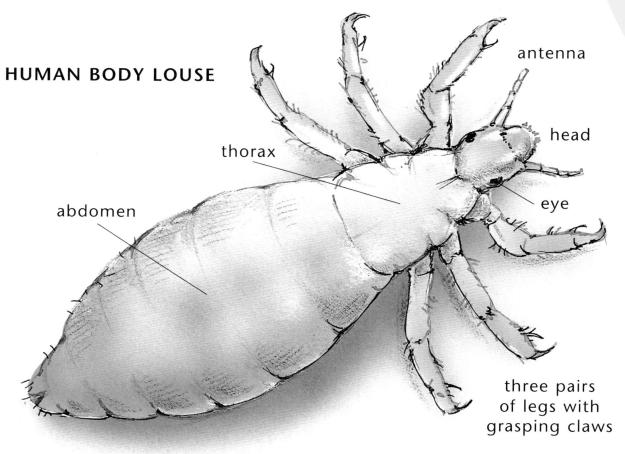

antenna

head

eye

thorax

abdomen

three pairs of legs with grasping claws

12

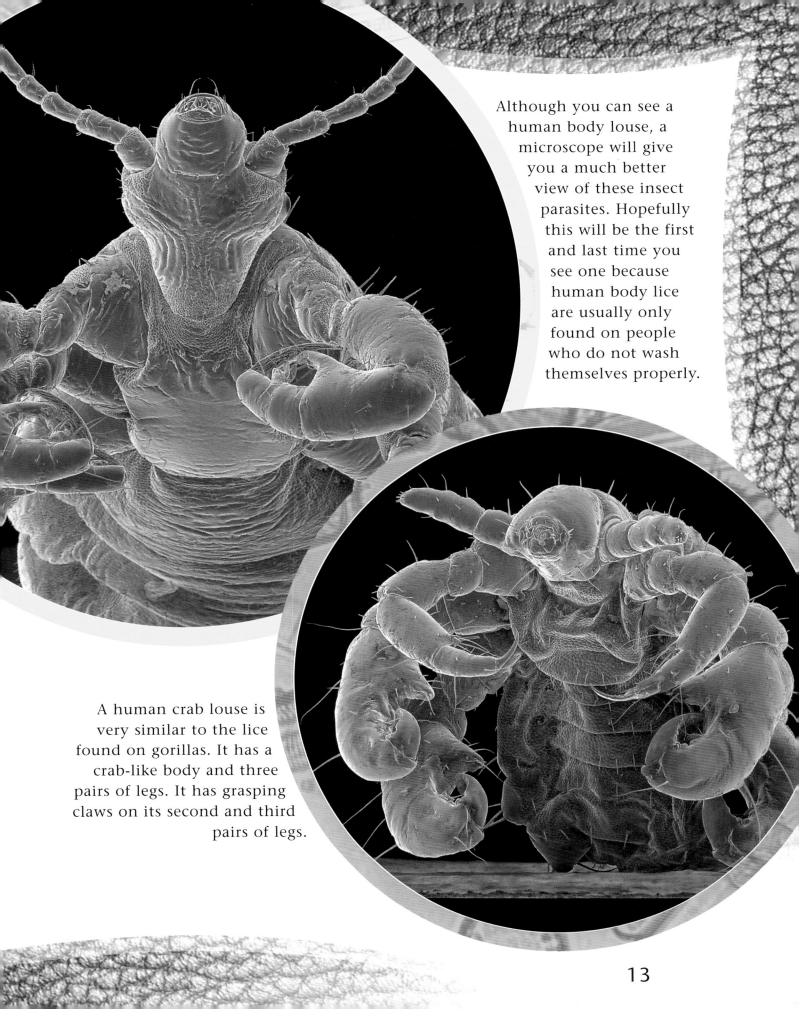

Although you can see a human body louse, a microscope will give you a much better view of these insect parasites. Hopefully this will be the first and last time you see one because human body lice are usually only found on people who do not wash themselves properly.

A human crab louse is very similar to the lice found on gorillas. It has a crab-like body and three pairs of legs. It has grasping claws on its second and third pairs of legs.

Burrowing mites

Scabies mites are less than half a millimeter long. They are so small that you can only just see them without a magnifying glass or microscope. Even though they are small, you would know if these mites were living on you. This is because they 'burrow' into a person's skin and cause an extremely itchy rash known as scabies. Similar mites cause a condition called mange in wild and domestic animals, such as pet dogs.

Scabies mites cannot live away from their human hosts for very long. They are spread by close personal contact, which means that scabies mites can sometimes infect a whole family. Scabies infections used to be common in older people, especially when they lived together in homes for the elderly. Modern treatments mean that scabies infections are now much less common.

Scabies mites are relatively easy to control with a chemical obtained from a pharmacist.

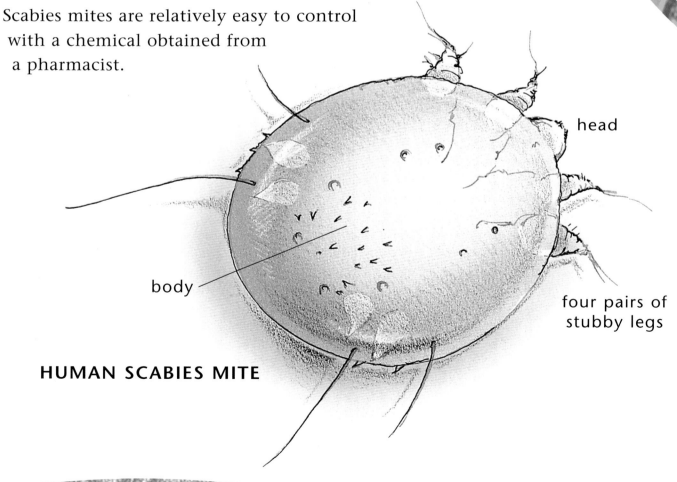

head

body

four pairs of
stubby legs

HUMAN SCABIES MITE

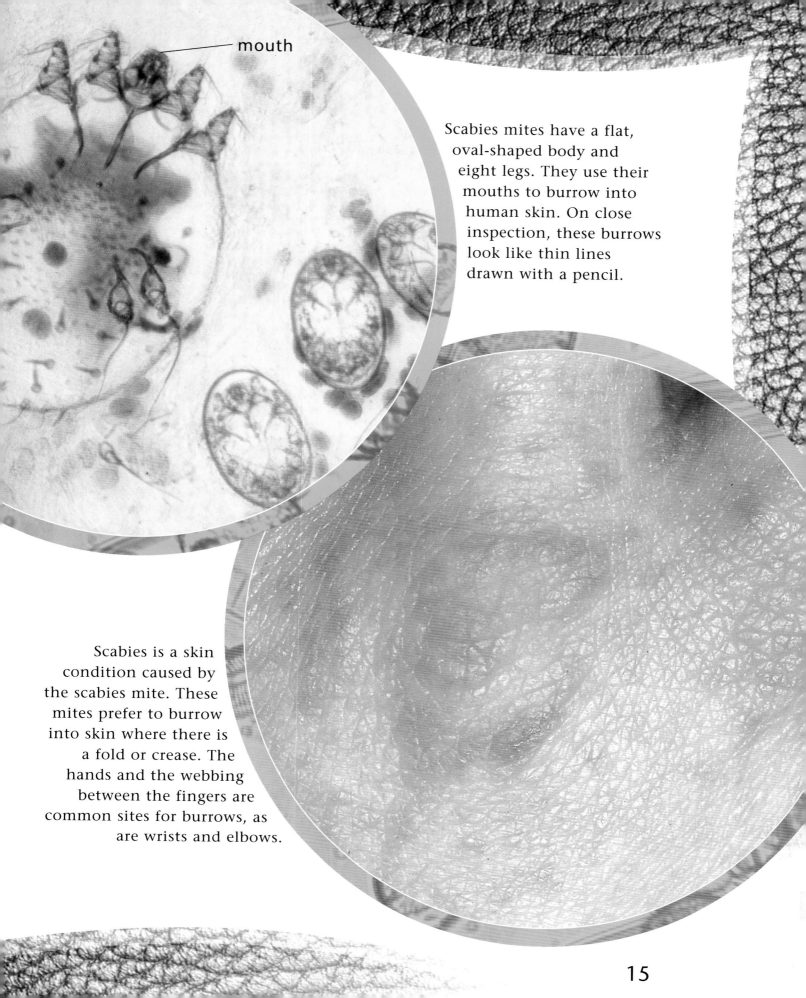

mouth

Scabies mites have a flat, oval-shaped body and eight legs. They use their mouths to burrow into human skin. On close inspection, these burrows look like thin lines drawn with a pencil.

Scabies is a skin condition caused by the scabies mite. These mites prefer to burrow into skin where there is a fold or crease. The hands and the webbing between the fingers are common sites for burrows, as are wrists and elbows.

Follicle mites

Like scabies mites, 🔎 follicle mites also make their homes in human skin. As their name suggests, follicle mites live in the hair follicles on our bodies. Hair follicles are tube-like structures within the human skin. Each hair follicle produces a hair, and has a gland that produces oil. There are actually two kinds of mites that live in human hair follicles. One lives in the follicle itself, and the other lives in the oil gland. This second kind of follicle mite is most commonly found in the hair follicles of the face, especially in the eyebrows. These are very common members of the human zoo and almost all people have these mites and do not even know it.

Follicle mites are even smaller than scabies mites. They are approximately a quarter of a millimeter (a hundredth of an inch) long. Because they have long, worm-like bodies, follicle mites are also sometimes called lard worms. However, follicle mites have eight short stumpy legs, so they are actually related to spiders rather than worms. As with scabies mites, follicle mites do not have eyes. They use needle-like mouthparts to feed on human skin cells. Unlike scabies mites, though, follicle mites do not burrow into the skin and they do not cause an **allergic reaction** such as a rash.

Human eyebrows and eyelashes are an ideal habitat for tiny follicle mites. Thankfully, though, these mites do not cause discomfort or itching.

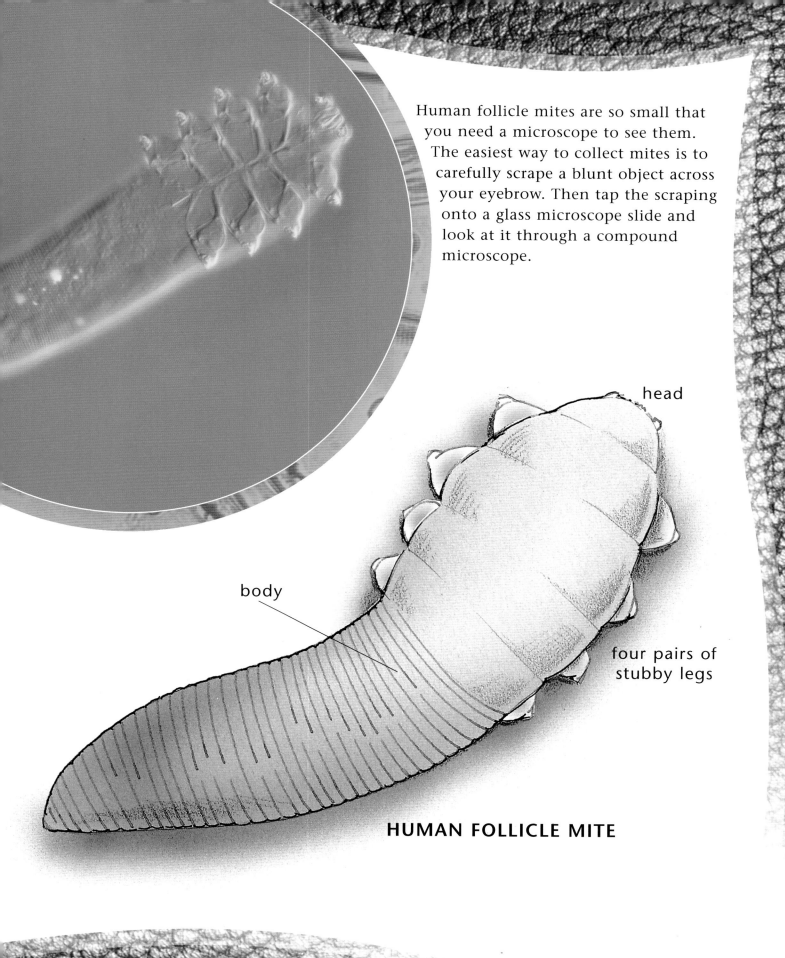

Human follicle mites are so small that you need a microscope to see them. The easiest way to collect mites is to carefully scrape a blunt object across your eyebrow. Then tap the scraping onto a glass microscope slide and look at it through a compound microscope.

head

body

four pairs of stubby legs

HUMAN FOLLICLE MITE

Bacteria and fungi

Countless millions of microscopic **organisms** (microbes) live on your skin. These microbes are either bacteria or ✈ fungi. Until ✈ Anton van Leeuwenhoek (see page 24) first used a microscope to study scrapings from his own teeth, we had never seen these tiny members of the human zoo. Nevertheless, the most suitable areas of your skin may be home to as many as 800,000 bacteria in an area as small as a postage stamp. In fact, the total number of bacteria living on your skin is probably greater than the number of people who have ever lived on Earth!

The bacteria and fungi that normally live on the skin are harmless. However, skin bacteria create chemicals that give you a distinctive personal odor. This personal odor is as unique as a fingerprint, but our noses are not sensitive enough to smell the differences between them. Changes in the normal bacteria and fungi that live on your skin may be quite noticeable, though. One example of this is known as ✈ athlete's foot. This itchy condition occurs when a skin fungus invades the warm and moist skin between a person's toes. A number of other itchy rashes and skin infections, including ringworm, are caused by fungi.

Bacteria are incredibly small—usually measuring only 1 micrometer across. They are able to survive in a wide range of inhospitable places, including human skin.

Mushrooms and toadstools that grow in fields are two well-known types of fungi. But there are other types of fungi that live on your skin. Some of these fungi are responsible for conditions like athlete's foot (shown here).

Yeast is another type of fungus that is found on human skin. Although much larger than a bacterium, each yeast cell is still very small—only one-tenth of a millimeter across. Like bacteria, yeast live on your skin in vast numbers.

Dust mites and ticks

As well as the wildlife living permanently on your skin, there are also many visitors. Most of these visitors share a number of features that help them to survive:

- they often have sensitive antennae that allow them to find a human host
- they are usually able to fly or jump
- they normally feed on blood that they extract from their host with sucking mouthparts
- they are generally able to survive for a long time without food but, when they do feed, they make it a big meal.

⚡ Dust mites are related to the other eight-legged mites that live within human skin. However, dust mites do not actually live on our bodies; instead they live in the fine dust found in our homes. Dust mites are especially common in beds, couches and carpets. Most of the dust on which they feed is made up of dead human skin. ⚡ Ticks are another type of eight-legged parasite, but that is where the similarity ends. Ticks can be quite large, and they live outside. Ticks can be regarded as members of the temporary human zoo because they feed on human blood.

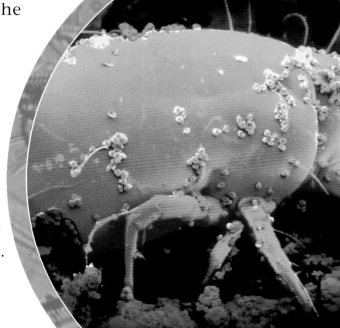

Dust mites are not a problem if they stay in place. However, if you breathe them in, dust mites can cause sneezing and asthma.

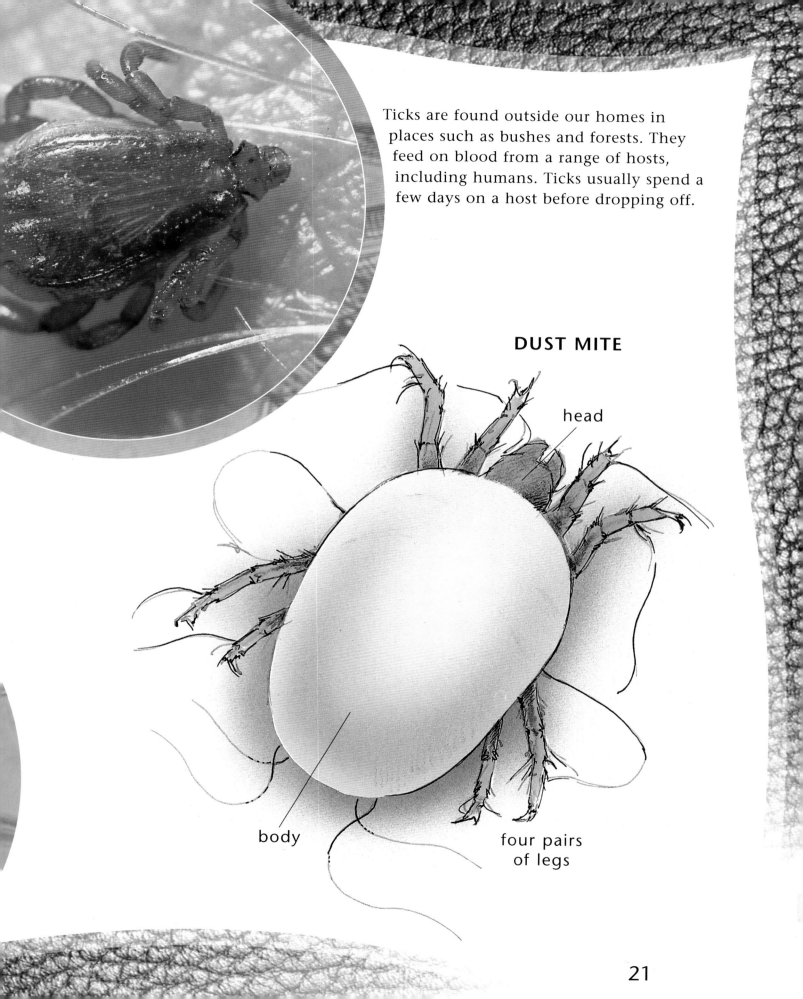

Ticks are found outside our homes in places such as bushes and forests. They feed on blood from a range of hosts, including humans. Ticks usually spend a few days on a host before dropping off.

DUST MITE

head

body

four pairs of legs

21

Fleas and bedbugs

⚹ Fleas are another temporary member of the human zoo. There are a number of different kinds of fleas, each closely associated with the home of their hosts. Modern human homes are generally very clean, so human fleas are far less common now than they were in the past. However, the fleas that pet cats and dogs bring into our homes can also feed on human blood. These flea bites can cause a lot of irritation and itching.

⚹ Bedbugs are also a temporary member of the human zoo. Bedbugs can live in mattresses and other soft furniture, and they come out at night to feed on human blood. Their bites cause itchy red spots that last for a few days. As with human fleas, though, bedbugs were far more common in the past than they are today. Thankfully, bedbugs cannot survive in a clean home.

A flea's back legs are long and well developed for jumping. Even though fleas are between 2 and 8 millimeters long, they can jump up to 300 millimeters.

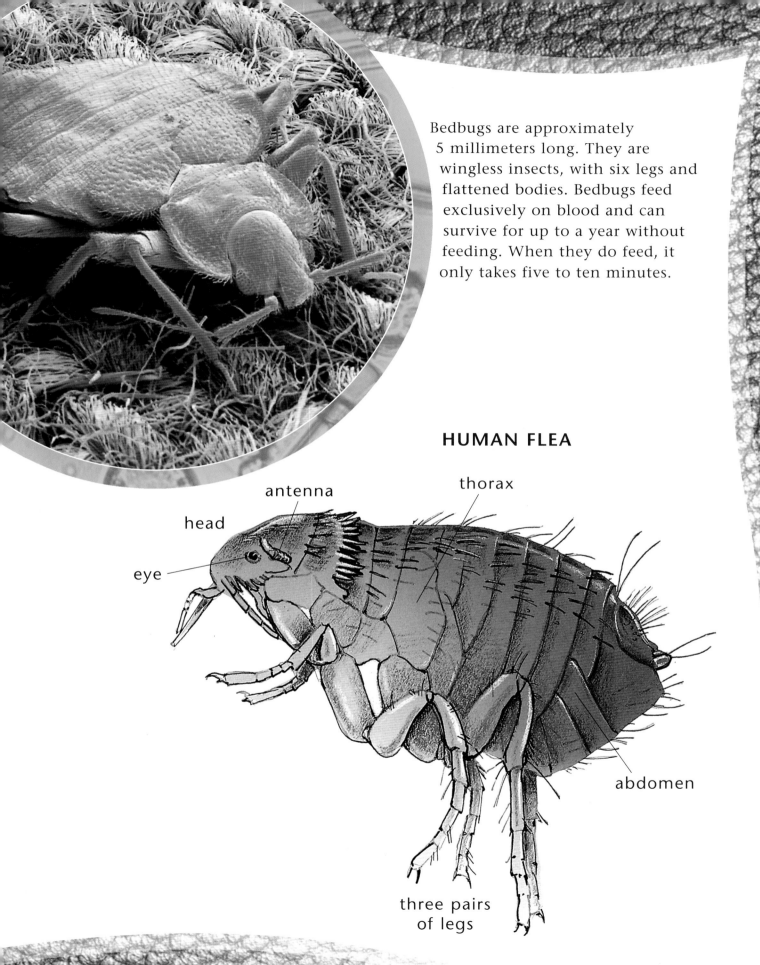

Bedbugs are approximately 5 millimeters long. They are wingless insects, with six legs and flattened bodies. Bedbugs feed exclusively on blood and can survive for up to a year without feeding. When they do feed, it only takes five to ten minutes.

HUMAN FLEA

head

antenna

eye

thorax

abdomen

three pairs of legs

Technology
Microscopes to view the human zoo

Because your personal zoo is so small, you will need a microscope to see all of these amazing organisms. All microscopes share one common element—a **lens** or series of lenses that make small things look bigger. The first microscopes were developed 400 years ago in the Netherlands (Holland). At this time, the Netherlands was the home of the first lens makers. They were making lenses for the first eyeglasses.

At least three of these Dutch eyeglass makers are credited with taking the lenses used for eyeglasses and using them to make the first compound microscope. They are ⚹Zacharias Jensen, his father Hans, and Hans Lippershey. Another Dutchman, ⚹Anton van Leeuwenhoek has sometimes been credited with inventing the microscope. However, he was born 30 years after the first microscopes were made. Leeuwenhoek is remembered because he made a simple microscope with a single lens that was powerful enough to let him examine the bacteria found in a scraping of **tartar** from his own teeth.

HOW DO YOU SAY IT?

Leeuwenhoek: **lee-an-hook**

Another type of microscope, called an electron microscope, uses a beam of electrons instead of light. One kind, called a scanning electron microscope, bounces this beam of electrons off an object to produce an image. Magnetic lenses are used to magnify the images made by the electrons. Scanning electron microscope images are three-dimensional, and very clear and detailed.

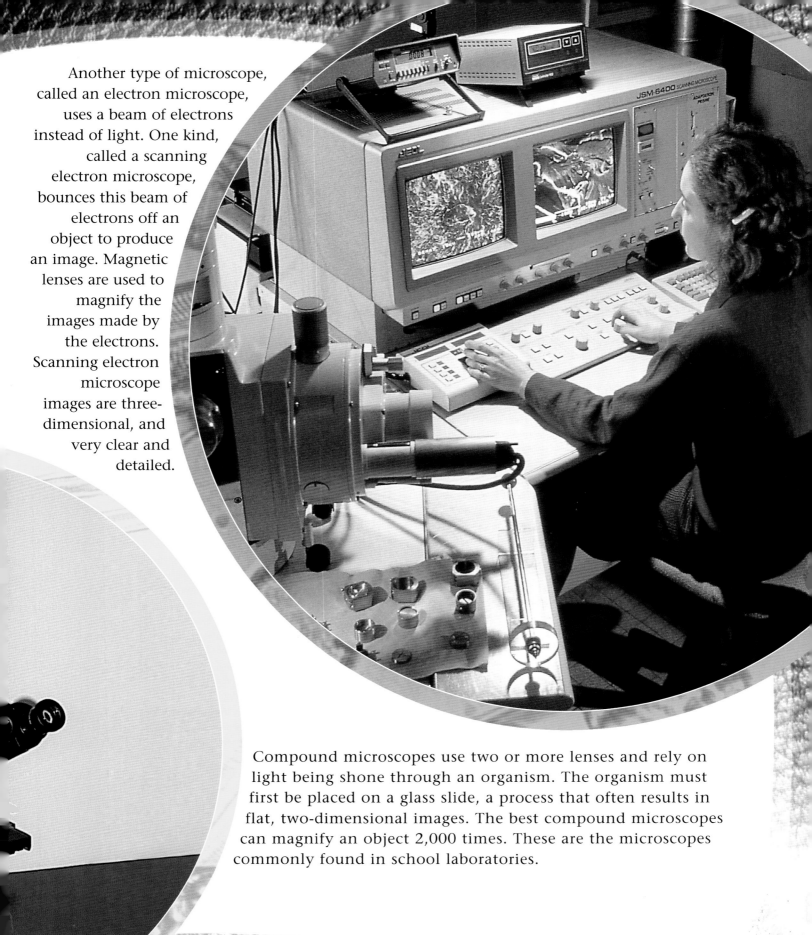

Compound microscopes use two or more lenses and rely on light being shone through an organism. The organism must first be placed on a glass slide, a process that often results in flat, two-dimensional images. The best compound microscopes can magnify an object 2,000 times. These are the microscopes commonly found in school laboratories.

Profile of a scientist
Professor Richard Russell

What happens when you think that you may have head lice or are bothered by some other member of the human zoo? The answer is that you should visit your family doctor or local health clinic. Doctors and other health workers are trained to recognize common members of the human zoo. They can also help you treat them. But what happens if your family doctor is not sure about the creatures that may be bothering you? The answer here is that your doctor would consult an expert. In Australia, one such expert is Professor Richard Russell. Professor Russell is a scientist who has worked as a medical **entomologist** for more than 25 years. He is the head of the Department of Medical Entomology at Westmead Hospital, in Sydney. Professor Russell specializes in the study of mosquitoes, diseases carried by mosquitoes, and the control of mosquito populations. He is also interested in both natural and artificially constructed wetlands.

HOW DO YOU SAY IT?

entomologist: **en**-toe-**mol**-o-gist
entomology: **en**-toe-**mol**-o-gee

A wetland is any area that is covered by fresh water to a depth of 6 meters (20 feet). Some wetlands are permanent and some are only temporary. Wetlands are sometimes called swamps. Professor Russell is interested in wetlands because this is where mosquitoes breed.

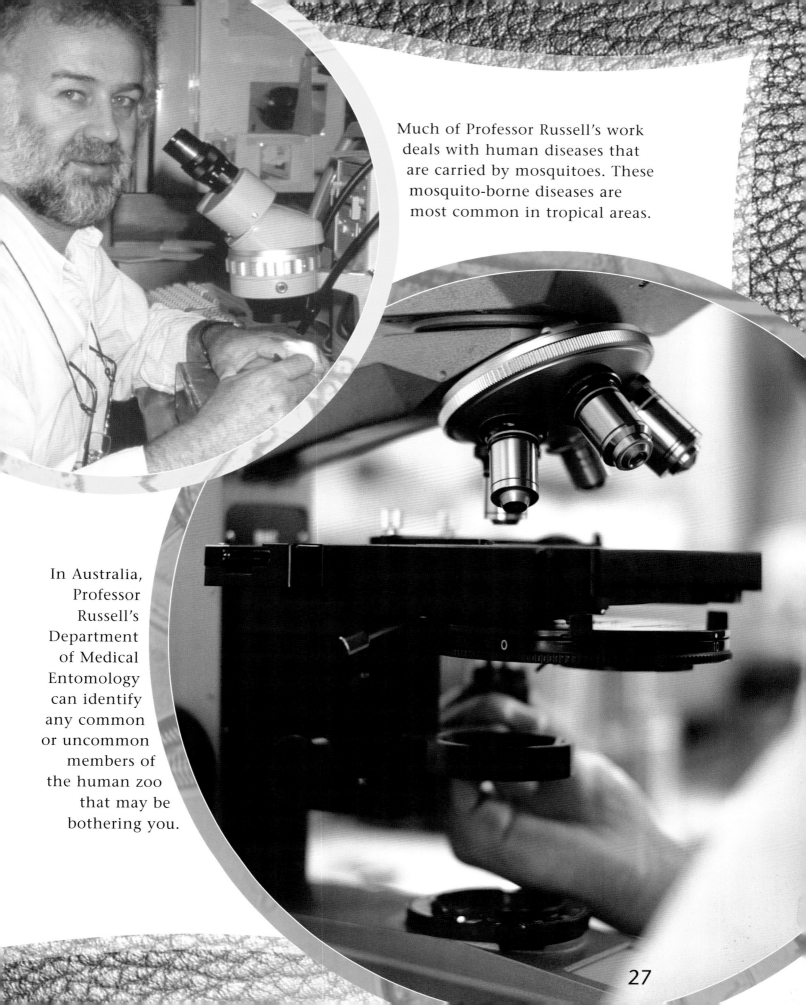

Much of Professor Russell's work deals with human diseases that are carried by mosquitoes. These mosquito-borne diseases are most common in tropical areas.

In Australia, Professor Russell's Department of Medical Entomology can identify any common or uncommon members of the human zoo that may be bothering you.

What the human zoo means to you
Parasites and human disease

It can be quite unsettling to discover that your body could be home to so many parasites. Thankfully, though, the zoo that could live on you is far more diverse than the range of organisms that actually do live on you. This is because most of the common parasites are restricted by our modern and hygienic lifestyle. Most of the human zoo that still survives is relatively harmless. Some, such as follicle mites, even thrive on modern skin creams and eye make-up.

This does not mean that all members of the human zoo are harmless. In the past, human parasites, especially fleas and lice, are said to have been responsible for more deaths than those killed in all wars. This is because fleas and lice carried fatal diseases, such as the plague and epidemic typhus. These diseases are still present today, but only in poorly developed parts of the world.

In the past, fleas have spread diseases such as the bubonic plague. This fatal disease, also known as the black death, killed over 200 million people in the 1300s. That was about one-third of the human population at that time.

Epidemic typhus is a disease spread by body lice. In the past (when humans usually carried a good population of body lice), it was one of the most deadly human diseases. It affected an estimated 30 million people during the early part of the 1900s.

Flying insects, such as mosquitoes, carry a variety of human diseases. One of these is malaria. Malaria is a tropical disease that affects hundreds of millions of people. It is caused by a blood parasite that is passed on to humans by anopheles mosquitoes.

Finding out more

Books like this one only give a brief introduction to a subject as broad as life on human skin. Some other useful reference books are:

Andre Deutsch, *Side by Side*, Andre Deutsch Limited, 1988
Anne Ingram and Peggy O'Donnell, *The Great Indoors*, Random House, 1995
John Downer, *Lifesense*, BBC Books, 1991
John Woodward and Casey Horton, *You and Your Home Under the Microscope*, Brown Packaging Books, 1996
Richard Conniff, 'Body Beasts', *National Geographic*, December, 1998
Theresa Greenaway, *Eyewitness 3D Microlife*, Dorling Kindersley, 1988

You may also find the following web sites useful:

medent.usyd.edu.au
This is the site of the Department of Medical Entomology at Westmead Hospital in Sydney (where Professor Richard Russell works).

www.dfwpest.com/human.htm
A web site about human parasites.

www.ifas.ufl.edu/~schoolipm/index.html
A site about integrated pest management in schools.

www.hsph.harvard.edu/headlice.html
A web guide to lice.

www.ghc.org/health_info/self/allergies/mites.jhtml
A web guide to mites.

www.capederm.com/info.htm
A web guide to skin infections.

www.uq.edu.au/nanoworld
A collection of microscopic photographs, including some of the human zoo.

As urls (web site addresses) may change, you may have trouble finding a site listed here. If this happens, you can still use the key words highlighted throughout the book to search for information about a topic.

Glossary

allergic reaction: A physical response or sensitivity to something that is normally harmless

compound microscope: A microscope with two or more lenses that makes an image of an object larger by passing light through it; this creates a color image

entomologist: A scientist who specializes in the study of insects and other small animals that affect human health

environment: All external conditions and factors, living and non-living, that affect an organism

habitat: The place where a group (community) of different organisms lives under a particular set of environmental conditions

hair follicles: Structures in the skin that produce hair

hosts: Organisms from which a parasite gains food

lens: A piece of glass or other transparent substance that bends light rays. Often used to create a magnified image of an object

metric system: A system of measurement that uses the meter as its basic unit

organ: A part of an animal's body that performs a special function. The skin is an organ

organisms: Living things

parasites: Organisms that live on (or in) and feed upon an organism of another species

scanning electron microscope: Also called a sem, this microscope uses a beam of electrons to make the image of an object larger. Sems produce a black and white image, but artificial colors can be added later if required

tartar: A hard substance left on teeth by saliva

yeast: A type of fungus

Index

579
BRE

DATE DUE

DEMCO 38-297